SILENCE - MAUNA

RASHMI MALAPUR JASWAL

Gratitude

I wish to thank my family, that is totally non-judgemental about my passion for writing poems.

Dedicated to

Meditators around the world and all those who find meditating almost impossible.

Contents

Contents

Foreword

In a world full of chaos that silences your voice, the basic human struggle has been reduced to getting one's voice heard. Finding your voice and getting it heard defines the struggle for existence. And then that old tale of assertion, glorifying the 'voice', and celebrating fights for that 'space' for one's voice rambles around everywhere, like noise pollution. In these cluttered chaotic voices comes the plea sprouting from the 'Silence', also known as 'Mauna'. Words sharply cut the glass of chaos, rather silently, and then negotiate the silence. This creative force filled with the meditative words of Rashmi, forms the poetic universe of 'SILENCE -MAUNA'.

Rashmi is a voracious writer with an uncompromising authentic attitude and relentless creative engagement with tasteful poetry. She never negotiated 'edits' and preserved her female spirit with a unique aesthetic. She always expressed herself without any filters, living ancestral visions of Lingayat saints like Akka Mahadevi. The commitment to 'originality' in her words reflects naked, ugly, dirty, spoiled, and affected feelings. Sometimes, it reveals fresh wounds with blood oozing out, and sometimes those permanent scars grow more pronounced when one gazes at them. Rashmi's earlier poetry flowed from traumas, hurts, mishaps, misfortune, derailments, and more. If one converts the metaphors to objective reality, one could find a clinical repertory of untreated psychological distress. She lived that chaos mindfully. It is a difficult terrain for a poet and poetry. It really hurts badly there! You can't live those feelings in an imaginary world. The 'pain' was not a typical creative imagination from South Mumbai. Rashmi revealed it as the jostling lived experience of Virar,

Nothing seems to settle

The voice within;

It's never in coherence with the noise outside.

Such a grip on reality is strikingly visible in the latest work of Rashmi. That relentless quest to unravel the inner core has surfaced in silence.

These poems are too random and rooted in a journey from chaos to consciousness. Imposing any literary barometer to view her work is a sin, because every poem opens up a new horizon. It affects the consciousness; it dismantles something stable inside you. The silence she has articulated is not bound by any structure, rhythm, or meaning. It comes in raw, fresh form in these 40 poems. She unlayered the silence with a feminine sense; she recovered it bravely from the chaos she had to live in.

The 'female' experience of chaos is inherently mysterious. The literature has often packaged it in different covers with feminist undertones. There is lyrical clamor and vivid imagery, and yet it has intimate tones that offer itself in the market. Rashmi's poetry symbolizes the reluctance to be lured by such feminist fetishization of chaos. Rather, she has entered into the realms of freedom and claimed the treasures of silence. Such rebellion makes her a poet with a gifted female spirit.

The universe is familiar with Osho's well-known tagline, "Silence shared in words." That truly holy consciousness, that place of inner silence and stillness, is phenomenally captured by Rashmi in her poetry. The encounters with death in 'Banaras', the forsaken free soul uncovered in

'Galaxies - Galaxy Within Me', and then the serene abodes in 'Nature' all open up a journey on a spiritual landscape. At the same time, Rashmi makes a point to highlight the other extreme, her 'being' thrown into the material world with 'Amidst Distraught', and then adds more evidence of existential drift in 'War'.

The soulful imagery of silence in its authentic shapes and layers is offered in 'SILENCE -MAUNA.' It lets you begin the journey with words trapped in the collection of poems and gradually takes you out of the world where words lose their meaning and everything sounds like 'Silence: The Mauna'. It is like the voodoo of a female shaman but here the shaman has become the silence herself. I hope this uniquely expressive collection provides you with a path to witness the power of the human soul to find the Silence within it.

Dr Govind Dhaske is a Social Work Educator currently functional at The University of Montana. He has a doctorate from prestigious Indiana University of Social Work. Dr Dhaske is a well-known researcher on hair symbolism and women's mental health. He is an amateur poet in Marathi.

Dr. Govind Dhaske charges words with meaninglessness and then argues with readers for their authentic interpretations. He is often found teaching students beyond any livelihood obligations and then seen everywhere writing with his unique positionality transcending disciplinary silos.

Preface

I thought of writing this book because whenever I've made an attempt to be silent, I have felt at peace. The clutter in my mind gets untangled and I gather energy to focus back to the present.

Being in the moment doesn't come naturally to me. It takes effort for me to live in the present.

I wrote some of these poems after meditating; some I wrote in a state of extreme chaos. Silence can stem from an unsettled mind and amidst disturbed surroundings. Being in a state of silence is the realisation that we need to slow down. Even though there is noise around, we are in a hurry to finish our work and are confused; the realisation that we have to slow down a bit to reconnect to ourselves is so important to ensure we are doing the right thing.

Slowing down gives our body cells, nerves and our mind, relaxation – we get hopeful even in the most hopeless situation.

Silence brings solace amidst the chaos.

I wish readers can relate to these poems that have sprung from my daily life. My attempt is to keep the expression and choice of words simplistic not denying that the poems are a journey from the conscious mind to subconscious mind and the journey back.

Silence is a stream that flows quietly and finds happiness in its rhythm.

I wish to take the opportunity to thank my family; my mother Pushpa Malapur, husband Devendra Jaswal, sister Mrs. Poonam Patil, friend Ashwin Balachandran and my coaches Mehul Dhulia and Vaishali Tare. They have stood by me in the toughest of times and believed in me.

1. Banaras

Something just dies within me each moment
And that's life.
Some words die,
Some breathes, too.
Blatantly screaming truths die
And a few bold thoughts, too.
Silence emerges as a result of these deaths.
Silence after a lifelong scream.
A wandering mind settles
After the chaos and a violent dream.

2. Chaos

I don't need you,
Yes, I need you.
Please wait,
No..no.. go away.
Morning tea with breakfast
Cooked by me.
Back to cooking lunch,
Then, the mad rush to be–
Words, words, and so much planning.
The chaos never ends.
My mind scurries for peace.
Amidst these chaotic moments,
Welcome a moment of inflection.
It's never about perfection –
All the madness comes to a still,
When you decide not consciously –
But something happens,
And you pause.
Amidst the chaos is your cause,
A cause to live,
Everything withers.
Chaos transforms
Gradually in your womb,
You give birth to SILENCE,
A treasure of a lifetime.

Though not eternal,
It has emerged from the chaos,
So detestable.

• 3 •

3. Staring at the Blank Canvas

The painter stared at the canvas,
Not knowing what to say;
Blankness called for colours
Silence calls for words.
In the blank canvas
Are hidden limitless colours
So is silence hidden
With emotions.. camouflaged perfectly
By serenity.

4. Deafening Noise

When the noise is deafening,
When time buries you,
Life just doesn't call you its own.
Only death lingers.
All that people say,
Is too loud.
All that you absorb is the shrill noise.
At the height of noise,
That you've been hearing,
Years have passed
But you've been bearing it.
Comes a moment of silence,
SILENCE…
You become deaf to every sound.
No matter where you go.
You've created a quiet world.
A peaceful abode,
Silence of this kind
Is beautiful;
It fills your heart with self-love.
A classic defence against the monotone.
The fierce tones,
Hurtful words,
Aren't piercing.
Only a serene silence prevails,

Upholding only one emotion:
LOVE…
Amidst the thorns and scorns,
The bloodshed,
Nothing matters,
But the fact that with SILENCE
You overcame so much more.

5. A Poem Made Me Silent

Once again, a poem came to my rescue
Once again, the world struck me
With a knife so sharp,
Wounded without bloodshed.
In pain without a tear.
Once again, it's a poem
That caressed me
Made love, set me free,
And silent.

6. What Stops You?

What stops you
Is within.
The force is intense
Your calm face,
A pretence.
Coming back to where you belonged,
You smelled so fresh at birth,
Got smothered with worldly love.
In moments of conflict,
Sitting at thy feet,
Nerves relaxing,
The splitting headache
Fading…
The sound of each breath so vivid.
Everything is crystal clear,
Water reflects your face.
Silence has resurfaced;
I longed for it,
I longed for you.

7. The Run for Silence

Scribbling on the desk of life,
It's getting nosier and blurry.
In a desperate attempt to gather
Whatever is hers.
The wind blows her mind away,
The sky falls on her.
In an attempt to lift it
She falls on her knees.
How humorous life can be.
The ocean tumbles her,
The mountain hides her,
Covered by nature,
She discovers herself,
Waking up from her dream.
The run for silence begins.

8. The Gathering

They all gathered
And began with a vote of thanks
Women said thanks to men,
Men to the women,
Children to the teachers
And teachers to their mothers.
They spoke, spoke and spoke.
At a moment when they stopped
They wondered,
If at all, we would choose to be silent.
We would connect to each one here.
Graced each one with affection
And not a fake smile.
There is no denying that
Words do a fantastic job.
But can there be a gathering
Where no one would say,
Everyone would just stay
Be there,
Be silent,
Feel the love and express,
Not with words
But with silence.

9. They Say

They say silence is serenity,
They say it is serendipity,
They say it's better to say it loud.
Lately, serenity scares me,
Lately, I'm scared of silence;
Scared of saying hello to me
And answering all the questions
That I have otherwise never asked.
Lately, it's been quite quiet.
Lately, you have been
There
Yet, not been around,
Away and distant,
It's been silent within.
As I breathe and focus,
Within its calm.
The scariness has led
To silence;
Silence that has nothing to do with serenity
Or spirituality.
It's acceptance – it's me,
That I fluctuate – that I rise and fall,
Wax and wane.
That I love standing on the beach
With open arms

And welcome the universe
And dissolve in silence!
Today, again there was a session arranged by Anita Risbood and it was extremely calming and soothing. I don't know if meditation is innately meant for this feeling, but at present, that is what I feel after each session. Thank you, Anita, for consistently conducting the meditation sessions each Thursday. I truly wish that you all join in and experience this awesomeness. Immediately after the session, I penned a poem for my book.

10. Galaxies - Galaxy Within Me

There is a galaxy within me,
So full of youth,
There is a voice within me,
So full of silence.
Encompassing all that was created
In the womb of the creator.
When I close my eyes
I feel the connection with
The outer galaxy
Merging in the full moon
With innate silence
A calm reverie
Dissolved in the almighty,
Complete truth and serene silence.

11. Settle

Nothing seems to settle
The voice within;
It's never in coherence with the noise outside.
Two voices
Simultaneously speaking at the same time.
Unable to quieten both,
Absorbing both
Makes me shun both lingering in my mind.
Irreparable damage,
I quieten within,
Silence is the only solace easily available
Yet tough to arrive at.

12. A Voice Within

Someone calls out to me
From the past,
From within,
A distant voice,
It's so sweet and soothing.
I wait for a minute,
Pause and rethink.
Solace is your presence
Or else nothing.
How do I live
Without you?
The long hugs and caresses
The memories that keep lingering.
Then, in a moment of solace.
I find peace,
Making peace with myself
And the world around
I suddenly break into a dance
Of madness, unbridled love for myself.
I dance my heart out,
Drenched in sweat,
I fall on the floor
Still and stable,
Feeling and hearing my own breath.
Everything is quietened,

Everything silent.

13. Amidst Distraught

In the midst of intense emotional distraught,
Sitting in silence embarks me on a journey within,
On the path of silence.
The beginning always has countless roadblocks of thoughts.
Each fighting with the other to seek my attention.
This war of thoughts leaves me famished.
But persistently facing the conflicts and not feeding them.
I do get wounded and bleed profusely.
The smell of the wet soil smudged all over my body lifts me up.
I take a deep breath,
Stay there for a while to experience solace and peace,
So rare in the continuously evolving world.
Something stays, and that is silence.

14. Violence

Violence takes over my mind,
Then, somewhere in the subconscious
Peeps a peakish stream
Flowing serenely through your eyes
And seeps deep into every part of our mutual existence,
And fills in the gap.
I gasp and hold you firm.
Silence stays in the underlying moments of extreme brutal violence,
As a cry of the conscience.
It is the cry to emerge as a human,
Overshadowed by animal instinct,
Trying to make its presence felt.
The stream of silence in the moment of violence.

15. Nature

Nature balances
Sound and silence;
It spreads love
Its abundant love fills
The universe with melodious music.
Its rage is ferocious,
Ensnarled by human violence,
Underlying currents of silence.
Retaining it,
Patiently waiting for wisdom and care.
Once attacked,
By thousand countless,
Hands of heartless humans.
From the shades of silence,
Emerges a shrill sound of temper.
Nature balances sound and silence beautifully.
Once the rage subsides,
Everything falls destroyed.
Silence spreads in a mournful cry,
Nature absorbs sound and silence alike.

16. Wisdom

Wisdom swelled into ego,
Thrashed and strangled by pride.
Silence is but a long pause,
To absorb all the might.
Absence of words,
Doesn't mean a lack of emotions.
Pause is graceful,
Silence blooms in a pause,
And a pause blooms into flowers of love.
It's a graceful expression,
Of nature and power within.
Will you give away your worlds,
And barter them for silence.
It's a wise deal,
Where ego is forsaken.

17. The Power of Words vs. The Power of Silence

Powerless, they say, are the wordless,
Mightier is the pen than the sword.
Used at a gathering
A vast congregation
Sly words slay the audience.
Though, silence is necessary and apt.
It is the attack of the mighty.
Ignoring all the noise outside and
The war within.
Overcoming the temptation of expression
Silence wins, and words fail.

18. You are Powerless Without my Reaction

Floating in the lightness of heart,
Surrendering myself to your limitless power.
I'm minuscule – a speck of dust,
On this vast expanse.
As I float, there is but silence,
That embraces me.
The moment I struggle to dismantle myself,
From the core of my existence.
Detach me from your hidden power.
I engage in a lost battle.
A perpetual fondness for a dismantled ego,
Disturbed, disinterested –
Hurt ego.
You know why the bird
Flutters in the cage?
Why does its shrill sound attack your silence?
And makes you weak?
Your mind is in a battle with itself.
Can't sit with your eyes closed.
Be an answer to this struggle.
Could you stop for a while and mingle?
With the divinity within you.
The moment of union,

Between the divine and the human.
They always were one.
But all the clutter
And the blaring noise –
Distance you from the divine.

19. A Sound of Rage at Times

It is the sound of the rage,
Don't perceive it as a forced profoundness,
Thinking is an inward journey,
Silence is not a destination.
But an act of putting all doubts at rest.
Putting your guard down,
Accept that erring is human,
And attack is not always the best defence.

20. As Night Falls

As night falls,
When the world sleeps.
Spreading a dead silence.
No birds chirping, no flowers blooming.
She immerses this mysterious universe in her womb.
Silence for some is scary,
For me, it brings back peace.
In this stark darkness.
In nothingness.
A gentle sound of breeze,
Caressing the leaves –
The pleasant breeze
Caressing me with love
Is the most endearing, soulful,
And peaceful.
End of many stories
Penned by the universe –
Thriving out of love,
For each creation.

21. Lovers Speak Endlessly

Lovers speak endlessly,
Till they feel utterly bored.
Then, silence overtakes all conversations.
As they sit hand in hand,
Staring at the sea,
Silently listening to the -
Melodious, rhythmic sound
Of the waves.
All the struggles of life,
Start to seem worthless.
Everything they said –
Is now pointless.
Silence has the power
To feel love –
Silence steps in -
When words die.
And just love prevails.
Questions fade
And love overtakes.
Silence is expressed through eyes
That don't lie.
The slow, deep breathes,
Felt in the womb of love,
And the eternal embrace.

22. A Cosmos Within

I'm on something
And I'm hardly up to it.
While reading a long article
I wished I would write this poem.
I'm on something
And I'm hardly up to it.
While I write this poem,
I wish to message someone.
I'm on something
And I'm hardly up to it.
Not a single thought
Stays with me,
Each one of them flutter.
My mind running -
Helter skelter.
Focussing; the toughest task.
Getting pulled,
In all directions.
Totally distracted –
A calm demeanour,
Is a pretence.
From within, I'm scattered,
Every such moment,
Is backed by a series
Of deeper breaths.

Closed eyes,
Accompanied by a calmer mind.
Silence becomes my companion
And I connect with myself –
In a meditative state.
Now calmer, composed and collected,
Quiet and tranquil.
Silence leads to
Preponderance of peace.
Yet to be explored
A cosmos within.

23. It's a Battle

It is a battle,
Certainly not simple.
The stark difference of opinion –
The mind is single.
With a dual voice.
Duality is always confusing.
Pulling you from all sides.
Tearing you apart.
When the noise,
Gets unbearable –
You shut yourself,
From all the noise.
And scream aloud –
Which deafens you,
For Silence to prevail,
And tears dissolve the pain.
Silence enters your life
And makes you a bit wise.

24. When Silence Spoke to Me

Silence once spoke to me
With a blaring noise.
Startled, I turned around,
To find out who it was?
I'm here the closest to you!!
Yet you refuse to notice me.
"Oh yes, the other day we met!!
You are silence.
Someone that I fret."
"Yes, I came to announce you,
As a being so wise.
Only if you wait and pause,
For a moment and rise."
As I did so –
Disquieted you were.
You slowly drifted away.
We departed then,
To quickly meet again.
Perhaps you need me.
And I feel the same.
I travelled miles to meet you,
Though I have been the nearest.
Your ignorance made everything pointless.

The moment riches stopped alluring you,
You shed the violence –
Self-inflicted by ignorance,
And walked into my arms.
I needed you as much
In pain, you were –
When the soul surrendered.

25. Silence at Our Doorstep

I have traversed across the cosmos,
Over centuries, they've pleaded
For me to settle with them for a while.
When I knocked on their doors –
They looked fierce and unable to hold
And welcome me in their lives.
The noise at the door was deafening.
They shut the door without recognising
What they hunted for so desperately.
So, I wandered in my aura, self-contained.
In no hurry, I learned to refrain,
From temptations to know their constraints.
Gradually, the universe played a trick,
The wiser species were in a fix –
They loathed life and lost their grip.
A series of aggressive nature's rage,
Caught them in a cage,
Bit by bit, they slipped and gauged,
At the past and they rummaged,
Looking at themselves and got discouraged.
The time was ripe, and then I hit a chord,
Among them, I came to rise.
A few of them learned to embrace,
The solace and became quiet.
My aura spread across,

The vast expanse of this universe,
Still absorbing, bringing peace.
While some still drive the force,
Attacking themselves with no remorse.

26. Music

Music is the sound of the divine.
Union of the body and the mind.
In that moment of fusion,
Everything dissolves.
You embrace nothingness,
Quiet and graceful,
Music gifts silence –
An unstoppable flow,
A stream of notes,
Seeping into the ravines,
Of your consciousness.

27. Monologue

I have been around
Since the universe was created.
Sounds, music and vibrations,
Sprung from me –
Yet today, I'm elusive.
Distant for some,
Deceptive for the abrasive.
How can I be resurrected?
Unearthed and respected.
When violence is at its peak.
The courageous become meek.
Layers and layers of mud get uncovered.
The truth is discovered.
Will I become one with the universe?

28. Sound of Bells

The sound of bells
Reverberating from a distance.
I suddenly wake up
To realise it's an illusion.
In a delusive state,
I go back and forth,
From the past to the future,
The bells ringing loudly.
Now I'm awake,
To hear them loud and clear.
I'm scared and fear,
The end of my faith,
That nothing can break.
I'm held by a strong force.
That emanates from within.
Assured it isn't a delusion.
I pause without a startle.
And move not a bit disgruntled.
In peace, I assimilate,
And absorb,
Silence is a befitting reward.

29. Dancing Shadows

Shadows in a dance revue,
Rhythmic movements that it drew.
The sky seems to rejoice,
From a distance, I heard a voice.
Words floating in the breeze,
I hear some, I lose some,
Breathing in the rhythm,
Of dancing shadows,
My feet start moving,
With a desire to uproot,
My distaste for everything,
That is natural and base.
Emerging from the sound,
Of my feet,
I start breaking,
The shackles of defeat.
My mind doesn't flounder
Silence but a divine wonder.

30. Aside

Drift away from the earthly
Move into the womb of silence,
The birthplace of strength.
Where life and creativity flower,
At your feet when they are offered,
Happiness is stirred.

31. Silence: A Solution

Infested intentions –
Everyone is in this,
Internal war.
Shoving the other,
Walking all over,
Trying hard to win,
To keep moving,
Is the only condition.
Survival the only ambition,
Thriving on violence,
Let's come together,
To fold our hands in silence.
Bow to the beautiful creation,
Bring back devotion into our lives,
Express our emotions.
Nothing needs to come to a standstill.
All that is needed,
Is silently pausing our violent actions.
Dwelling in peace within,
Curiously looking,
At the universe in consciousness.
Assimilating mindfully,
The ocean of wisdom,
Gathered over the years of existence.
Silence –

Is being in a state of nothingness,
A thoughtful pause
Could be the only solution.

32. War

What are we doing here?
Said the child in the arms,
Of her mother,
Sloshed in blood,
Hit by weapons of destruction,
Attacked by the enemy in venom.
Unending differences,
Placed against each other,
In the name of religion,
Two beautiful lands,
Holding on to their facts.
Killing each other,
Unable to explain,
The growth of civilisation.
Decades of destruction,
Destabilisation lives,
Of potent creation.
Regressing and unremorseful,
Devastating consequences,
War culminating into a catastrophe.
The solution is distant,
Decades of discussions,
Conflicts triggered by unwavering faith.
The core of human existence –
Is co-creation.

In war is unending destruction.
If only faith could bring peace,
And force us to.
We all would agree
To practise communion of silence.

33. Lovers Meet

They met at twilight and united,
Struggled to keep their faith,
In their love for each other,
Intense, fearless and forceful.
Bringing love and devotion,
In their deeper emotions.
They must have met even before,
Past life regression if you believe in -
So, when they met,
They spoke in silence.
Silence is the language of love,
Bringing back together lovers across lives.

34. Breathing in You

A detailed wishlist,
That keeps adding up,
Among these is the desire to sit in silence.
With you for long,
Longing for nothing,
Asking for nothing.
Breathing with you,
Breathing in you.
Knowing you closely,
Fitting perfectly in your arms,
You are so close yet distant,
Blooming and blossoming,
Living in you,
Me and you,
Are one in two.
Breathing with you,
Breathing for you.

35. Harmony

Aggressive breathes are nursed,
Amidst complete silence,
Healing bit by bit,
The mind calms and
The body relaxes.
A state of complete tranquillity,
Reigns on the mind, body and soul,
Shedding prolonged state of conflict –
Fluster and furore are replaced with harmony,
Attaining a state of balance and inner peace.

36. Anxiety

An anxious mind,
Can never think straight.
It fluctuates fiercely
Oscillates violently.
Getting a hold of yourself,
Becomes a task.
Watch your breath,
Let nature take its course.
The rhythm of your breath,
Will make you happy.
Becoming the source of harmony,
A flow of soothing music,
Calming every string,
Bringing peace,
Instilling self-belief.

37. The Present World

Disturbing are the challenges of the daily world.
Mundane, routine and lacking deep involvement,
Social media is a frivolous world,
A reflection of contrived existence.
While we barely survive in this obnoxious world,
We don't abhor the frivolity,
Instead, embrace it.
Life continues to haunt us,
Not with bigger challenges,
But worries that are fickle.
Adding to this frivolity,
Is the unending desire,
To be acknowledged socially.
The lack of sensitivity,
Towards the need of consciousness,
Mindfulness is a rarity.
If we collectively sit in silence,
Ditching the superficial,
And look deep within,
It would render peace and,
A deep sense of fulfilment.

38. Source of Energy

Shining upon you,
A light that seeps through,
That lights up,
Your present moment,
That carves your future.
The source of energy,
In the midst,
Of existential crisis,
A cry of hope,
Valuing the natural
Flow of life!!

39. Song of Silence

Bringing back,
Gushing through,
Is a flow,
Stopping its force.
Slows you down,
Immerse in it,
Flowing like a river,
In silence.
Growing on you,
Each moment of life,
Is a live force,
Trembling with excitement,
Don't resist the energy,
Live in it,
Immerse in it,
Flow like a river,
In silence.
Rooted to the ground,
Raw in energy –
Growing bit by bit,
The mud is smudged,
On the pulse of life.
Live in it,
Immerse in it,
Flow like a river,

In silence.

40. Numb

My mind is numb,
Shut to the noise outside.
Everything that hits it,
Bounces off and never returns.
For long I have absorbed
All that needed no attention.
Distractions fluttered my mind,
Could never fix my gaze.
Stillness brought by meditative moments,
Immersed in myself –
Away from the outer world.
Being with myself,
Became the joy of life.
A calm demeanour,
And a quintessential smile.
Peace eluded many,
In this crowded world.
Silence brought peace,
Mind that calms
After a war of thoughts.

www.ingramcontent.com/pod-product-compliance
Lightning Source LLC
Chambersburg PA
CBHW040110150726
48005CB00013B/1645